Jenny Speaks Out

Sheila Hollins
Valerie Sinason

Illustrated by Beth Webb

St George's Mental Health Library
LONDON

First Published in Great Britain 1992
by St George's Mental Health Library,
Cranmer Terrace, Tooting, London SW17 0RE
Series Editor: Professor Sheila Hollins

ISBN 1 874439 00 1

British Library Cataloging - in - Publication Data

A catalogue record for this book is available from the
British Library

Typeset, printed and bound in Great Britain by
HGA Printing Company Ltd, Brentford Middlesex

Other titles in The Sovereign Series:
When Dad Died
When Mum Died
In preparation:
Bob Tells All
Peter's New Home
A New Home in the Community

Available by mail order from:
The Division of Psychiatry of Disability
St. George's Hospital Medical School,
Cranmer Terrace, London SW17 0RE

Dedication

To all those people with learning disabilities who have shared their experience of abuse with us.

Acknowledgements

With thanks to the following whose interest and encouragement has made this book possible:

Members of the Division of Psychiatry of Disability at St George's Hospital Medical School, and of the Tavistock Clinic and Foundation.

Jenny, John and Mary were friends. They moved to a new house together.

Kay helped them settle in.

John chose his own curtains,
carpet and furniture. He put
his treasures by the window.

Mary chose her furniture.
She put her old teddy on the
bed. She liked her chest of
drawers best.

Jenny didn't want to make
her room comfy.
She stayed outside.
Her room was still empty.

"Why haven't you chosen anything for your room yet?" asked Mary. "It looks horrible," said John.

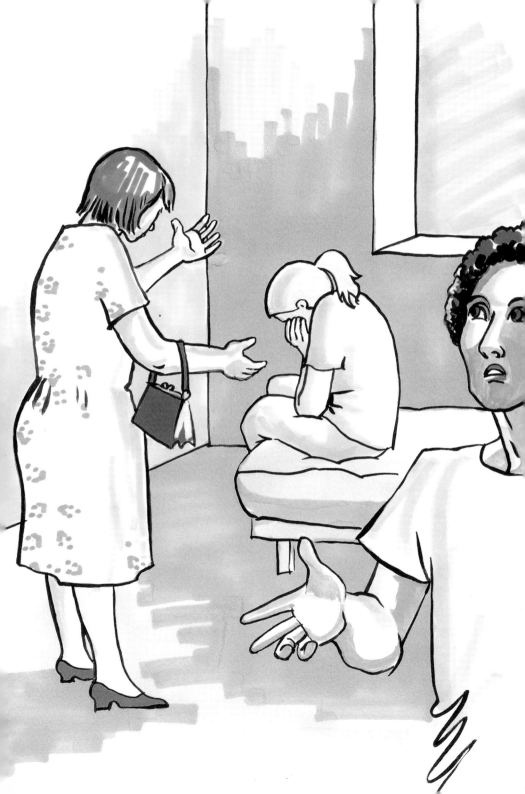

Kay asked Jenny: "Shall I help you unpack?"

Jenny ran to the corner of the room. She sat on the floor and cried and rocked.

"What's the matter?" asked Kay. Jenny wouldn't answer.

Kay picked up a photo from the case. "Is this your Mum and Dad?" she asked.

Jenny snatched the photo
from Kay. "I hate it!"
she shouted.

Jenny bit her fingers and hit her head against the wall. Mary and Kay were worried.

"What's the matter?" asked
Kay. "Is it your Mum and Dad?"
Jenny said nothing.
Kay thought for a moment:
"Is it your Dad?"

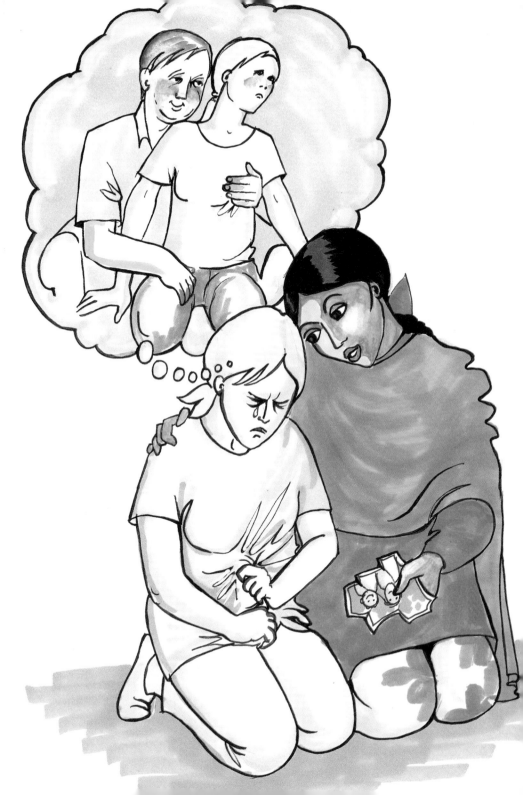

"Yes!" shouted Jenny.

"Can you tell us?" asked Kay.

"Dad said it's a secret," said Jenny.

"It makes me feel dirty and I can't speak about it," said Jenny.

"You don't have to keep bad secrets," said Kay and Mary. "You can say what you want to."

"It's my Dad. He came into my bedroom at night and he hurt me. It keeps going round and round in my head."

Jenny pointed between her legs. "He hurt me here," she said. "I feel dirty."

"I hate him," Jenny said.
"I'm glad he's dead."

"How terrible!" said Kay.
"Poor Jenny, now I understand."

John knocked on the bedroom door. Kay asked Jenny, "Can John come in? Its up to you who comes into your room."

Jenny said, "Come in John.
Thank you for knocking."

Jenny cried again. She asked Kay to tell John her story.

They sat on the floor together.
Mary said Jenny's Dad had
done dirty things to her.
That was why her bedroom
frightened her.
John said he knew about
things like that.

Jenny was lucky to be
starting her new life with such
good friends.

Jenny brought her things inside and made her room comfy.
Kay said Jenny had been brave to tell and they would talk about it some more.

BEYOND WORDS
counselling people with learning disabilities

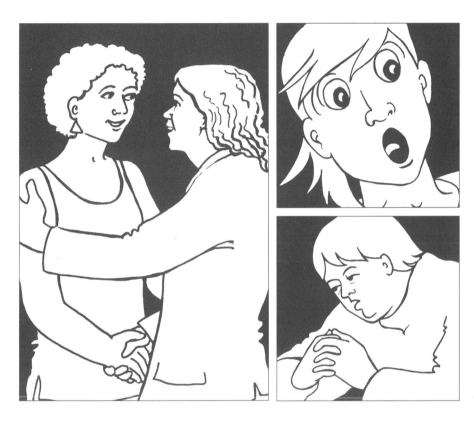

Editor: Professor Sheila Hollins

Illustrations and Design: Beth Webb

These beautiful books from St. George's Mental Health Library explain the difficult things of life to adults with learning disabilities. They also help carers to talk about sensitive topics. The books communicate powerfully but gently, through colour, mime and symbol providing an effective and invaluable counselling tool.

BOOKS BEYOND WORDS have been carefully designed to support the emotional development and counselling of people with learning disabilities.

The books deal with subjects that the Series Editor, a Professor of Psychiatry of Learning Disability, and her co-authors, who are Senior Practitioners have found to be crucial: for example, disability, dependency, sexuality and mortality.

These full colour picture books provide an effective and invaluable counselling tool, assisting people to adjust to change, to accept themselves, to enable them to have satisfying relationships and to make their own decisions.

They also help carers in finding a way to deal with sensitive topics. The books also offer the 'reader' a positive direction and reassurance for the future. People with learning disabilities enjoy owning their own copies.

Books Beyond Words utilise special techniques of non-verbal communication, blending emotionally keyed colours, body language, mime and symbols. The effect of this is to speak clearly to the 'reader', explaining difficult and painful experiences with 'language beyond words'.

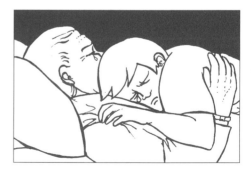

Books in Print

Each of the following books is one of a pair in which the same theme is explored with different people or in a different setting.

Jenny Speaks Out (1992) / Bob Tells All (1993)

Sheila Hollins and Valerie Sinason.

Shortlisted for Book Trust and Joseph Rowntree Foundation 1994 Read Easy Awards.

These books are designed to enable a person with learning disabilities to open up about their experience of sexual abuse.

*Hug Me – Touch Me (1994) / Making Friends (1995)

Sheila Hollins and Terry Roth.

* Winner of the Book Trust and Joseph Rowntree Foundation 1994 Read Easy Awards in the best author category.

Janet (in Hug Me – Touch Me) and Neil (in Making Friends) want someone to hug, but they always pick the wrong person. These two books tell the story of how each learns when they can and can't hug or touch.

When Mum Died / When Dad Died 2nd edition (1994)

Sheila Hollins and Lester Sireling.

Shortlisted for Book Trust and Joseph Rowntree Foundation 1990 Read Easy Awards (1st edition).

Each of these two books tells the story of the death of a parent. Gently and straightforwardly, the events of death are presented and the feelings of grief are experienced.

Peter's New Home / A New Home in the Community (1993)

Sheila Hollins and Deborah Hutchinson.

Shortlisted for Book Trust and Joseph Rowntree Foundation 1994 Read Easy Awards.

For people with learning disabilities moving home can be a frightening experience. Proper preparation is vital for a happy transition. In Peter's New Home, Peter leaves his family to go to a group home. A New Home in the Community tells how Simon leaves a hospital where he has lived for many years.

continued over

Going To Court (1994)

Sheila Hollins with Valerie Sinason and Julie Boniface.
This book is about a victim who is helped to be a witness in a Crown Court.
The pictures are designed to fit any crime and any verdict.

You're Under Arrest (1996)

Sheila Hollins with Isabel Clare and Glynis Murphy.
What happens if you are accused of a crime? This book takes the accused step
by step through the police procedures.

You're On Trial (1996)

Sheila Hollins with Glynis Murphy and Isabel Clare.
This book continues the story of You're Nicked, from being charged to
becoming a defendant in a Magistrates' Court. It introduces all those involved
and offers a range of alternative outcomes.

Feeling Blue (1995)

Sheila Hollins and Jenny Curran.
Ron loses interest in eating, swimming and
other activities he usually enjoys. He becomes
irritable and withdrawn. Feeling blue shows
what happens to Ron when he is depressed,
and how he is helped to feel better.

*B*EYOND WORD*S*
counselling people with learning disabilities

Order form available from
Mrs Freda Macey, Department of Psychiatry of Disability,
St. George's Hospital Medical School, Cranmer Terrace, London SW17 0RE, UK.
TEL: 0181 725 5501 FAX: 0181 672 1070 e. mail: s.hollins@sghms.ac.uk.